ANGEL CARVING

AND OTHER FAVORITES

RON RANSOM

PHOTOGRAPHY BY GEORGE A. CLARK

Schiffer Publishing Ltd

1469 Morstein Road, West Chester, Pennsylvania 19380

DEDICATION

TO THE MANY CARVERS WHO HAVE ENCOURAGED ME TO DO THIS SECOND
BOOK. THANKS, I HOPE YOU HAVE FUN WITH THESE ANGELS AND OTHER
FAVORITES.

Printed in the United States of America.
ISBN: 0-88740-147-3
Published by Schiffer Publishing Ltd.
1469 Morstein Road, West Chester, Pennsylvania 19380

This book may be purchased from the publisher.
Please include $2.00 postage.
Try your bookstore first.

FOREWORD

The things we do in the name of love. I first began whitling in 1969 after my wife, on a trip to Mexico, had admired a carving of a monk and I had boasted that I could do the same thing. I could not, of course, but the attempt launched me toward what turned out to be a magnificent obsession, and, with the exception of one career-dominated hiatus, I have found that few things give me as much pleasure as the creation of wood figures.

Ron Ransom, who wrote and directed the illustrations in the book you are about to enjoy, was similarly influenced by Cupid when he carved his first Santa Claus as a special present for his wife, Evelyn. While our motivation sprang from the well of purest emotion, our preoccupation with carving over the ensuing years must have left our wives filled with all the gratitude of a golf widow whose husband has promised to get his handicap down to six in her honor.

Fortunately, this little scam works as well for females as for males. If Ron's latest tome on how to carve Santa, angels and Noah's Ark figures causes you to abandon the dishes in the sink or the leaves in the gutter, your partner will surely forgive you when you display your latest creation. And you may be as fortunate as Ron to have your carvings in such demand that you can actually justify your obsession with frequent contributions to the family petty cash reserves.

I have read many books on wood carving, but none have been set forth with such easy-to-follow text and pictures as I have discovered in Ron Ransom's first book, "Santa Carving", and in this, his second book. While the instructions are ideal for beginners, even advanced carvers can pick up a few new tips—not to mention some terrific patterns from a master whose special little figures are becoming a favorite with collectors around the country.

One final note of personal gratitude. It was encouragement from Ron and delight drawn from his first book that inspired me to sharpen my knives and begin to carve again. It is one thing to admire an artist's work, but even greater to gain inspiration from him. I believe this book will have a similar effect on anyone with the desire to create.

Lee Walburn
Editor
Atlanta Magazine
Atlanta, Georgia

INTRODUCTION

I have been delighted with the response from my first book, "Santa Carving." I have found that there were a great number of carvers like myself who could use a little help and a few ideas. I have enjoyed your letters, phone calls and even a few visits here in Marietta, Georgia. The letters from excited wives who have gotten their husbands off the couch and carving a few Santas have been special.

Your comments have made it a little easier on this second book which I had no intention of doing. You have asked for additional views and I intend to give you as many photos as I can afford.

These subjects I have chosen are favorites of mine and I hope you will try a few. You have made me hustle and carve more types of Santas. Some of these I will share and continue to encourage you to experiment with the designs and add your own personality.

Noah's Arks have been popular toys for years and lately have become very collectible. Many years ago the Ark and animals were the only toys allowed on the Sabbath. Many varieties were made with the greatest number being made in East Germany.

My first memory of angels was in the reading of the Christmas story. Angels are mentioned a number of times. I have researched books on weathervanes and found quite a few angels. Our carving ancestors found the angel to be a good subject for weathervanes and a few can be found in folk art collections. It was thought that the angel brought good luck and in some instances was used for religious reasons. I offer you the same deal I did in "Santa Carving." If you don't understand a carving or want more information, write me at; Box 4101 Marietta, GA 30061—enclose a stamped, self-addressed envelope.

Good Carving
Ron Ransom

GETTING STARTED

I'M USING THE WAYNE BARTON CERAMIC SHARPENING STONES

I've met one person who said he enjoyed sharpening knives. He was on his way to our state mental institution as a guest.

Almost every carver I've talked to has a different way to sharpen knives. If I put every gadget and stone on my workbench that I've purchased to sharpen with, I wouldn't have room for anything else. Through trial and error I've settled on the method shown here. I've found the inexpensive Woodcraft knife and the Knotts knife to be as good as any to sharpen and hold an edge.

Above shows the dark Barton Stone which is good for the first step which is getting the dullness off the metal. Do not hold the blade at too steep an angle as it will create shoulders. I hold my knife almost flat. The photo on the right shows the Fine grit stone.

Push the blade away, then turn the knife over and pull toward you along the stone. After what seems a long time the wire edge should start to show.

In the photo below—I switch to the smoothest water stone and continue to sharpen both sides—push away—bottom right—pull towards you.

I made my leather block with two pieces of thick leather. I put the rough side on one side of a 1" piece of wood and the smooth side on the other side—Of course, I glued them on. I rubbed some medium grit compound on the rough side. . .

. . .and continued the push, pull sharpening notion. The wire edge should begin to disappear now.

If this doesn't look like the smooth side of the leather it's only because I couldn't find the right photo. The final honing is done on the smooth leather.

If you want to get into some serious sharpening I recommend *Sharpening and Knife Making* by Jim Watson.

Other than using the leather strop on my electric drill, this is my sharpening paraphernalia. I've found the Dico tripoli compound works well on the leather strop as well as the flat leather. If you can read Japanese, I'm sure the entire directions for sharpening are on the end of this waterstone.

ANGEL #1

YOU MAY WANT TO LOOK AT THE COLOR
PHOTO OF ANGEL #1 BEFORE YOU START.

CARVING .
INSTRUCTIONS

THIS IS ANGEL #1. IF YOU DON'T WANT TO CUT
UP YOUR BOOK, COPY THE PHOTO AND GLUE
TO INDEX PAPER. CUT OUT AND YOU'RE
READY TO TRACE ON A 1" PIECE OF
BASSWOOD. IF YOU'RE NOT GOING TO DETAIL
THE FACE THEN KNOT FREE WHITE PINE WILL
DO.

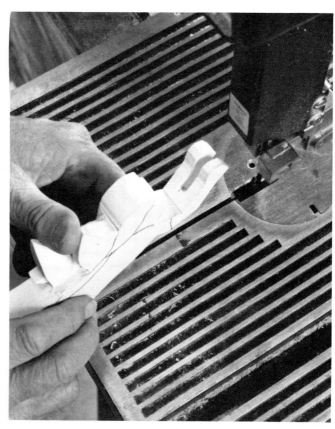

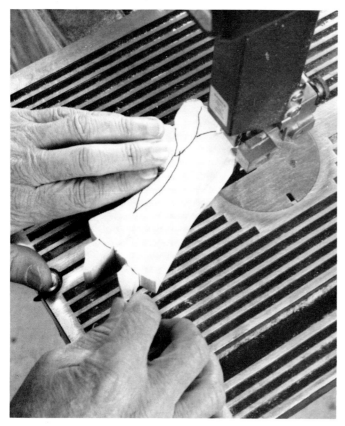

CAREFULLY CUT OUT THE ANGEL.

CUT A NOTCH BETWEEN THE HANDS.

INCISE OR SCORE IF YOU WISH THE DRAWN LINE. I USUALLY CUT IN ABOUT 1/16 OF AN INCH.

BEGIN TO ROUND AND SHAPE. REMEMBER, MOST NEW CARVERS TEND TO LEAVE THEIR WORK TOO SQUARE.

THAT OLD, FAT THUMB OF MINE IS
IRREPLACEABLE. MY RIGHT WRIST IS LIKE IT IS
HINGED AND THE LEFT THUMB FURNISHES
THE STRENGTH NEEDED TO MAKE THE CUT.

YOU MAY MAKE THIS ANGEL SEASONAL BY
CHANGING THE WREATH AFTER CHRISTMAS
TO A HEART FOR VALENTINE OR IF YOU
REALLY WANT TO MAKE FRIENDS, HANG A
HUGE DIAMOND RING OR A ROLEX WATCH
ON THE HANDS. IT WORKS FOR ME.

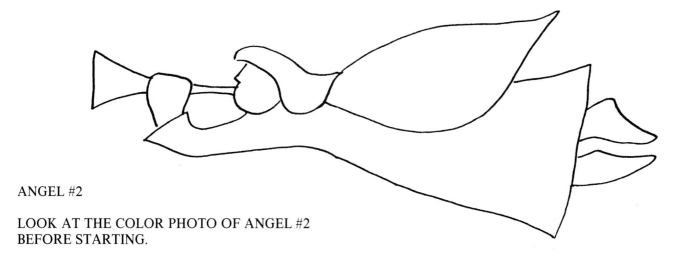

ANGEL #2

LOOK AT THE COLOR PHOTO OF ANGEL #2
BEFORE STARTING.

A REMINDER—LOOK AT THE COLOR PHOTO.
TRACE THE ANGEL ON A PIECE OF 1"
BASSWOOD.

CAREFULLY, CUT OUT THE PIECE.

YOUR PENCIL IS AN IMPORTANT TOOL. DON'T BE AFRAID TO USE IT. HERE, I'VE MARKED A CENTER LINE ON THE WINGS.

I'VE INCISED AROUND THE HAIR AND OTHER DRAWN LINES. THIS CUT WILL ALSO MAKE A PLACE FOR THE GOUGE TO STOP.

THIS IS THE FIRST TIME I'VE SWITCHED TOOLS OTHER THAN A KNIFE. A SMALL GOUGE WORKS WELL HERE. IF YOU DON'T HAVE A GOUGE, THEN MAKE A CUT DOWN THE CENTER OF THE WINGS AND CUT AWAY THE WASTE.

AGAIN, THE TRUSTY PENCIL SHOWS WHERE THE ANGEL FINGERS WILL GO.

HERE I'VE ROUNDED THE HEAD AND HAVE TAKEN SOME WOOD OUT OF THE HORN. IF YOU CAREFULLY DRILL THE END OF THE HORN IT IS EASIER TO GET SOME WASTE OUT.

THIS PHOTO SHOWS THE ROUNDED HAIR AND ARMS A LITTLE BETTER.

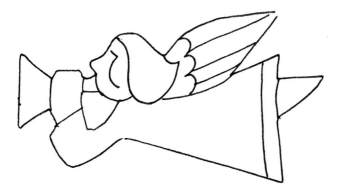

ANGEL #3

ALTHOUGH IT IS THE SMALLEST I THINK
YOU'LL FIND IT A REAL CHALLENGE. A
WARNING. . . PUT ON A DECENT PRICE IF
YOU'RE GOING TO SELL.

THIS IS ANGEL #3 AND WILL TAKE ABOUT AS
LONG AS THE OTHER TWO ANGELS.
LEFT PHOTO SHOWS THE PATTERN
TRANSFERRED TO A PIECE OF 1" BASSWOOD.
UPPER RIGHT PHOTO SHOWS THAT YOU ARE
ONLY CUTTING THE TOP SIDE.

DRAW A LINE DOWN THE CENTER OF THE ANGEL AND *CAREFULLY* CUT IN HALF, NOW YOU HAVE TWO ANGELS.

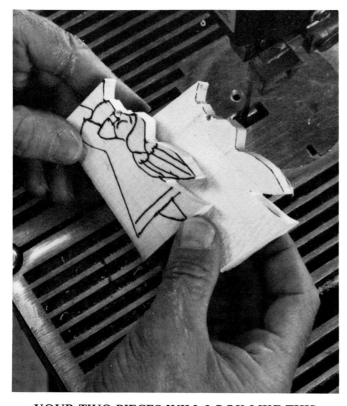

YOUR TWO PIECES WILL LOOK LIKE THIS.

PUT A SMALL SPOT OF HOT GLUE ON THE ENDS AND CONTINUE SAWING THE PIECE OUT.

INCISE YOUR LINES

BEGIN ROUNDING THE EDGES. REMEMBER
THIS IS AN EXTREMELY SMALL PIECE. DON'T
TAKE BIG CHUNKS.

CONTINUE TO ROUND

CUT A LINE DOWN THE MIDDLE OF THE
WINGS. AT AN ANGLE, CAREFULLY CUT AWAY
UNTIL YOU HAVE A NICE SEPERATION
BETWEEN THE WINGS.

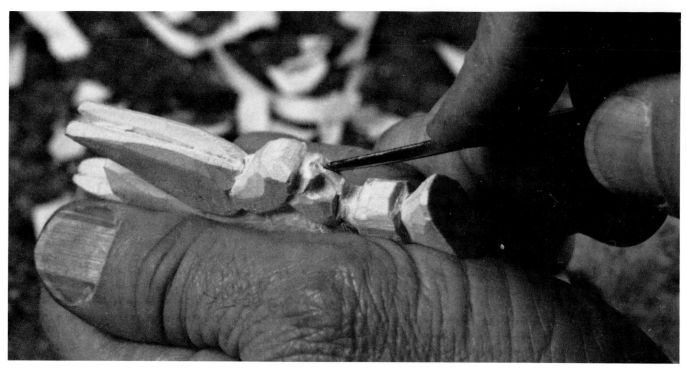

A DETAILED FACE IS REALLY NOT NECESSARY.
IF YOU WANT ONE, A SMALL VEINER IS
HELPFUL.

YOU MAY EITHER CUT IN THE WING DETAIL
OR BURN IT IN.

ANGEL #4

TRACE THE PATTERN FOR ANGEL 4 ON A 1"
THICK PIECE OF BASSWOOD. THIS DESIGN
LENDS ITSELF TO PLAQUES. THE DESIGN IS
SIMPLE AND SHOULD BE EASY TO ENLARGE.

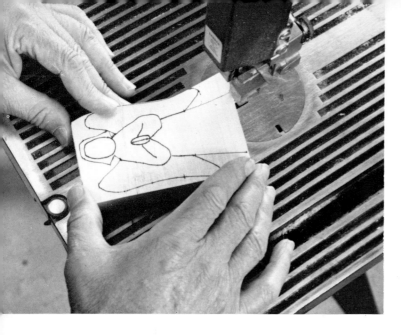

CAREFULLY, CUT THE PATTERN. THIS ANGEL IS BIG ENOUGH TO CUT WITH A SABRE SAW WITHOUT CUTTING YOURSELF.

INCISE THE LINES ON THE FRONT

AND THEN. . .

INCISE THE LINES ON THE BACK. DON'T WORRY ABOUT GOING TOO DEEP.

START ROUNDING THE WINGS AND ROBE.
NOTICE THE THUMB HELPING. MY THUMB IS SO
FAT IT SOMETIMES GETS IN THE WAY. I TRIED
TO EXERCISE, BUT IT STAYS THE SAME SIZE.
SERIOUSLLY, I COULDN'T GET BY WITHOUT IT.

CONTINUE ROUNDING BOTH SIDES, FRONT
AND BACK.

BE CAREFUL AROUND THE HAIR AND
SHOULDER. THE WINGS HAVE TAKEN SHAPE
AND THE PRAYING HANDS HAVE BEEN
DEFINED.

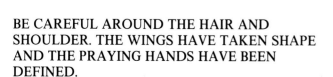

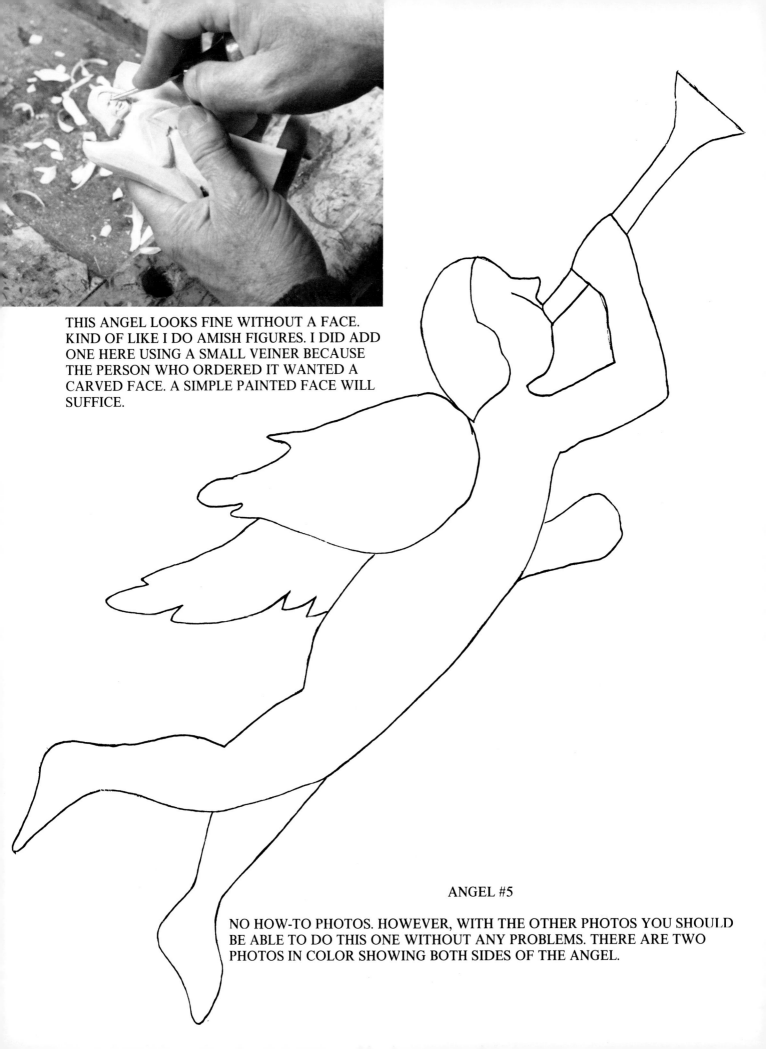

THIS ANGEL LOOKS FINE WITHOUT A FACE.
KIND OF LIKE I DO AMISH FIGURES. I DID ADD
ONE HERE USING A SMALL VEINER BECAUSE
THE PERSON WHO ORDERED IT WANTED A
CARVED FACE. A SIMPLE PAINTED FACE WILL
SUFFICE.

ANGEL #5

NO HOW-TO PHOTOS. HOWEVER, WITH THE OTHER PHOTOS YOU SHOULD
BE ABLE TO DO THIS ONE WITHOUT ANY PROBLEMS. THERE ARE TWO
PHOTOS IN COLOR SHOWING BOTH SIDES OF THE ANGEL.

ANGEL #6

TAKE A LOOK AT THE COLOR PHOTO BEFORE YOU START THIS ANGEL

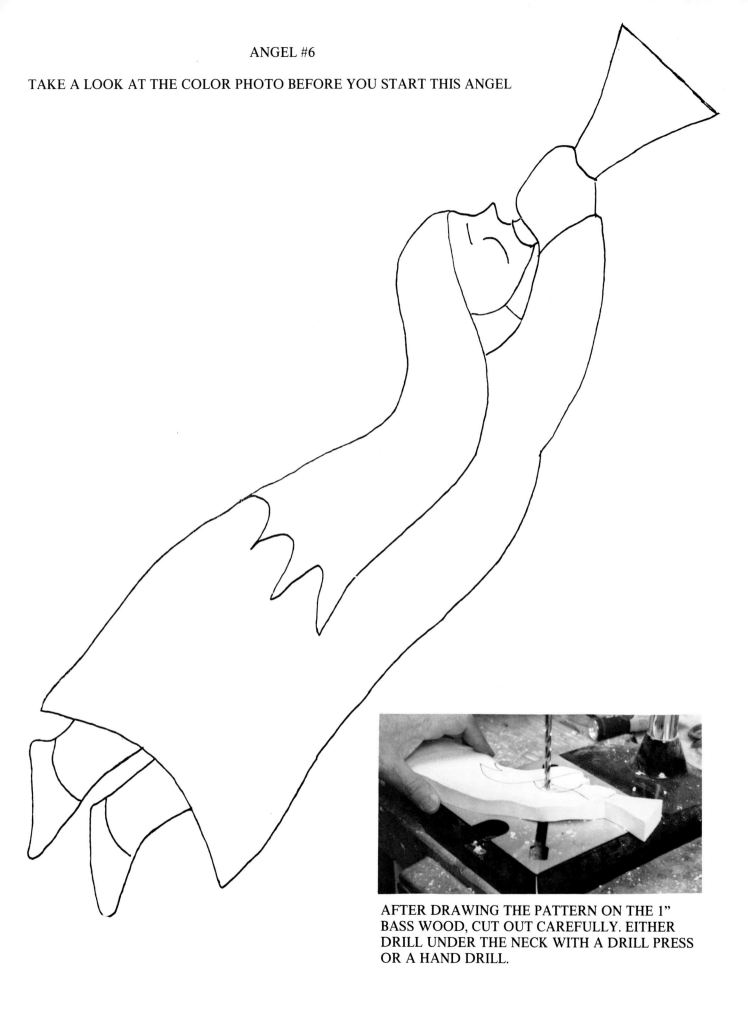

AFTER DRAWING THE PATTERN ON THE 1"
BASS WOOD, CUT OUT CAREFULLY. EITHER
DRILL UNDER THE NECK WITH A DRILL PRESS
OR A HAND DRILL.

IF YOU'VE DRILLED A LARGE ENOUGH HOLE,
YOU CAN GET A SABRE SAW BLADE IN AND
CUT TO THE LINE.

IF NOT, TRIM IT OUT WITH YOUR KNIFE,
ROUND THE EDGES, MAKE THE HORN ROUND
AND PUT SOME DETAIL IN THE HAIR AREA,
LOOK AT THE COLOR PHOTO FOR DETAIL.

NOAH'S ARK ANIMALS

GRAIN

THESE LITTLE ARK ANIMALS ARE A PAIN TO
CUT OUT. ON EACH OF THEM I LEFT THE
BOTTOM FLAT AS I DID ON THE SMALL ANGEL
(GO BACK AND LOOK) SO I COULD CUT IN
HALF AND HAVE THE NECESSARY PAIR.
REMEMBER, THESE ANIMALS ARE PURE FOLK
ART AND MOST PEOPLE WILL NOT WANT TO
CHECK THE ANIMAL'S PLUMBING TO SEE IF
THEY ARE MALE OR FEMALE. LOOK AT THE
COLOR PHOTOS TO SEE HOW I DID THE ARK
WITH ANIMALS FOR THE GRANDCHILDREN TO
PLAY WITH.

BROWN HAIR OR
WHATEVER YOU LIKE

RED NOSE
PINK CIRCLES

SKIN COLOR

DOTS RED

RED

WHITE

RED

RED STRIPES

BLACK

ANN

FACE COLOR SAME AS ANN

BLUE

WHITE

SHIRT BLUE & RED
STRIPES

BLUE

RED STRIPES

BLACK

ANDY

TRACE THE PATTERN ON THE 1" THICK BASSWOOD

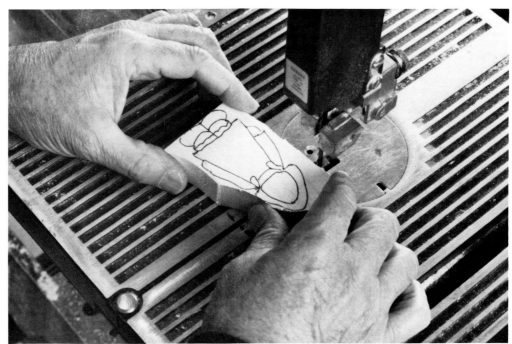

CAREFULLY, CUT OUT.

START TO ROUND AND AFTER INCISING YOUR LINES ON THE DRESS AND OTHER AREAS, CUT GENTLE LINES. YOU WILL PAINT MOST OF THE DETAIL, SO DON'T WORRY ABOUT MAKING YOUR LINES TOO DEEP.

CONTINUE TO ROUND AND CUT SCALLOPS IN
THE DRESS. ROUND THE FACE.

TRACE ANDY ON 1" BASSWOOD.

CAREFULLY, CUT OUT—THS IS A SMALL
PIECE—KEEP YOUR LITTLE FINGERS OUT OF
THE WAY.

KEEP ROUNDING—AGAIN, REMEMBER YOU WILL BE PAINTING THE FACE ON. YOU'LL WANT IT TO BE SMOOTH. THE PHOTO BELOW SHOWS ROUNDING THE FANNY AND CUTTING THE LINE BETWEEN THE LEGS.

DUE TO A MENTAL LAPSE, I DID NOT GET A PHOTO IN COLOR OF THESE TWO. I HAVE HAD THEM CAST IN THE PECAN SHELL STUFF. IF YOU ARE INTERESTED IN HAVING A SET, DROP ME A LINE
BOX 4101, MARIETTA, GA 30061   OR GIVE ME A CALL (404)971-0238

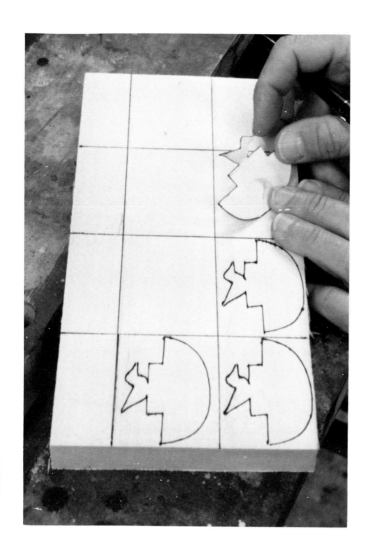

NOAH'S ARK AND DOVE

LEFT PHOTO. PLAN TO CUT OUT SEVERAL—
THESE HAVE BEEN AN EXCELLENT SELLER.

BELOW. CUT OUT THE BIRD SIDE OF THE ARK.
LEAVE THE BOTTOM FLAT.

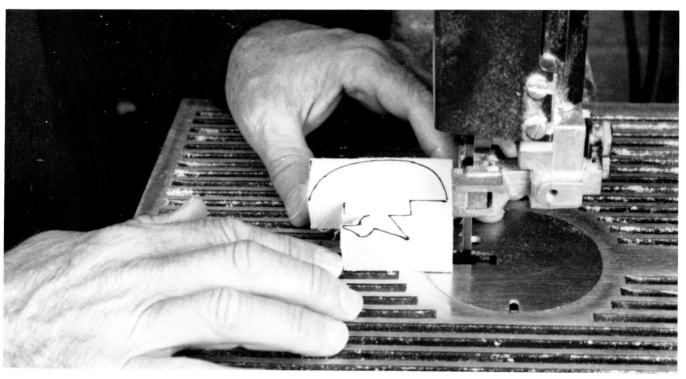

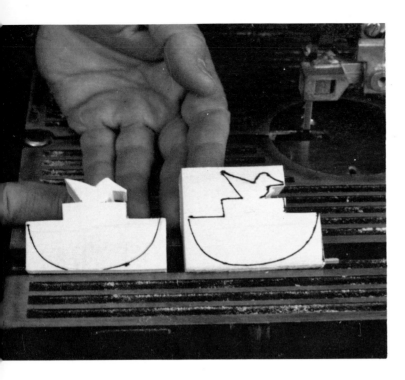

YOU HAVE COMPLETED THE FIRST STEP. MOVE
TO YOUR DRILL PRESS OR YOUR HAND DRILL.

RIGHT PHOTO SHOWS WHY ENDS WERE NOT
CUT. DRILL A HOLE FOR THE RIBBON TO BE
RUN THROUGH LATER.

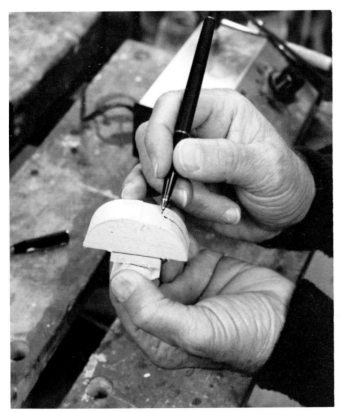

AFTER CUTTING THE BOTTOM LINES, DRAW A
CENTER LINE ON THE BOTTOM OF THE ARK.

DRAW IN UPPER DECK. THIS WILL HELP WHEN
YOU START CUTTING.

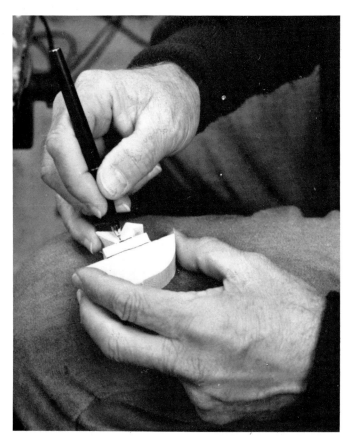

(1) OUTLINE THE DECK AND CABIN AREA

(2) OUTLINE THE DOVE

(3) START ROUNDING THE ARK

(4) I'M CARVING TOWARDS MYSELF CARE-FULLY, DON'T TRY UNLESS YOUR THUMB IS LEATHERY.

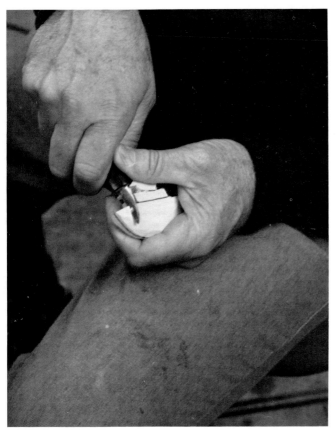

(1) TRIM TO WHERE YOU MADE THE LINE ON THE DECK

(2) START TRIMMING AWAY THE WASTE ON THE DOVE. NOTICE THE THUMB.

(3) CONTINUE TO SHAPE THE BIRD. BE CAREFUL WITH THE BEAK.

YOU'RE ALMOST THERE WITH THE DOVE.

(A) I HARDLY EVER SAND, BUT I'VE FOUND THESE LITTLE ARKS WILL WOOD BURN BETTER IF THEY ARE SANDED.

(B) USE A STRIP OF EMERY CLOTH AND GENTLY PULL UNDER YOUR THUMB WITH LIGHT PRESSURE.

(C) AFTER THE ARK IS SMOOTH, BURN A DOUBLE LINE ABOUT 1/16" WIDE.

THIS WILL GIVE YOU AN AREA TO BURN YOUR DECK TO.

(A) BURN PARALLEL LINES ON BOTH SIDES OF THE ARK.

(B) DRAW LINES VERTICALLY SO THAT IT LOOKS LIKE BOARDS.

(C) START TO BURN IN THE DECK.

(D) BURN THE DECK ON BOTH SIDES.

(A) BURN IN THE PORTHOLES.

(B) *CAREFULLY*, BURN THE BEAK.

IT'S AMAZING SOMETHING THIS SMALL TOOK
SO MUCH TIME. THE FIRST TIME I DID BRAIN
SURGERY IT WAS THE SAME WAY.

TREE SANTA (A)

SHOWING THE BACK OF THE TREE SANTA (A).

CUT OR BURN DETAIL INTO TREE.

FLYING WEATHERVANE SANTA (B)

I'M PUTTING THE FLYING SANTA ON A 1¾"
PIECE OF BASSWOOD. THIS MAY BE TOO THICK
FOR YOU. IF SO, PUT YOUR DESIGN CLOSER TO
THE BOTTOM. CUT THE TOP PART OF DESIGN
AND THEN CUT IT THE THICKNESS YOU LIKE.
REFER BACK TO THE LITTLE ANGEL FOR THE
DIRECTIONS.

THIS DESIGN WAS IN "SANTA CARVING" BUT
THERE WERE NO CARVING INSTRUCTIONS OR
A PATTERN. MANY OF YOU ASKED TO HAVE IT
INCLUDED. HERE IT IS. THIS ONE TAKES AS
LONG AS ANY I HAVE CARVED.

CAREFULLY CUT OUT YOUR SANTA.

INCISE THE LINES. IT LOOKS THE SAME ON BOTH SIDES. SO TURN IT OVER AND DO IT AGAIN.

ROUND COMPLETELY. MAKE CUTS BETWEEN ARMS, LEGS AND FEET. CLEAN OUT THE SLIVER AND ROUND TO THE AREA WHERE THE SLIVER WAS. (IF THAT MAKES SENSE GIVE ME A CALL. I DON'T UNDERSTAND).

NOTICE THAT I'VE ROUNDED THE HORN AND BAG AND SHAPED THE LITTLE BALL ON HIS CAP. TAKE IT SLOWLY ON THE LITTLE BALL. IT WILL FLIP OFF IF YOU PUT TOO MUCH PRESSSURE ON YOUR KNIFE.

BORE A SMALL HOLE IN THE HORN AND TRIM
OUT. THE FACE IS A CHALLENGE DUE TO THE
FACT IT'S AT THE END OF THE CUT.

THIS PHOTO GIVES A GOOD SHOT OF FACE.
THE SANTA MAY HAVE MITTENS OR YOU CAN
CUT SOME FINGERS. THERE ARE TWO GOOD
VIEWS IN COLOR FURTHER ON.

WALKING SANTA (C)

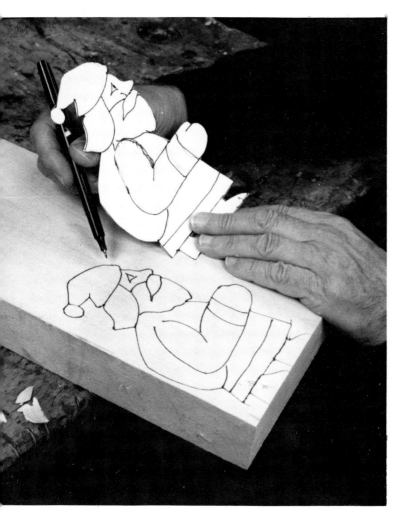

TRACE YOUR DESIGN ON 1¾" BASSWOOD.

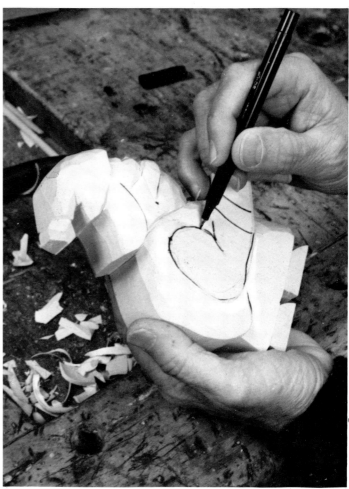

BEGIN TO ROUND THE BAG AND SHOULDERS.

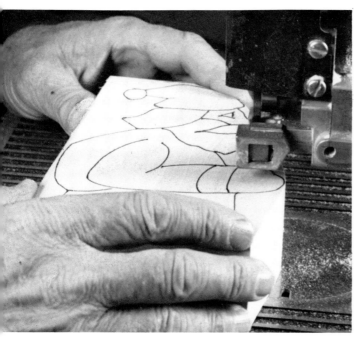

CAREFULLY, CUT OUT YOUR SANTA. INCISE YOUR LINES.

START TRIMMING THE BEARD.

TRY A FISHTAIL GOUGE FOR MOVING A LOT OF WASTE.

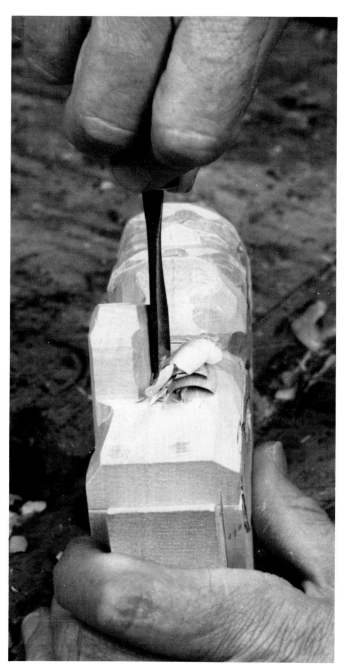

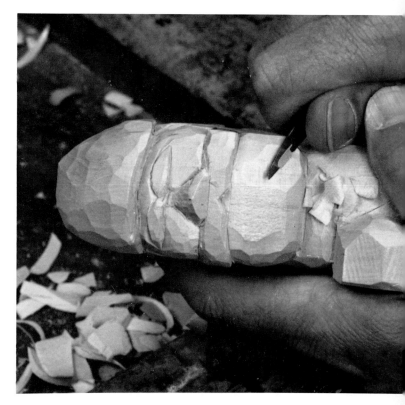

DEFINE THE FACE. BE CAREFUL WITH THE
EYEBROWS. THEY WILL POP OFF.

DON'T TRY THIS IN YOUR LAP. THERE ARE
ENOUGH TENORS IN THE WORLD.

DON'T BE AFRAID TO CUT AWAY FROM THE
NOSE AND MAKE IT PROMINENT.

WALKING SANTA (D)
THERE ARE TWO VIEWS IN COLOR.

I WAS INSPIRED TO DO THIS
SANTA WHILE BABY SITTING
WITH MY TWO-YEAR-OLD
GRANDSON. HE WENT
TEARING DOWN THE HALL
WITH ONLY HIS PAJAMA TOPS
ON. HIS FAT LITTLE BUNS
WERE SO CUTE I DECIDED TO
DO THIS SANTA IN HIS HONOR.

THIS SIZE ALSO GAVE ME A
GOOD DESIGN FOR THE SMALL
PIECES OF BASS WOOD I HAD
LEFT OVER. OH, YES—HE'S
SELLING EXTREMELY WELL.

ADD BEDROOM SLIPPERS IF
YOU WANT.

NIGHT AFTER CHRISTMA SANTA (E)

DRAW YOUR PATTERN ON ANY 1¾" PIECE OF BASS WOOD.

YOU DON'T HAVE TO DRAW THE BACK NOW. WAIT TILL YOU HAVE THE FRONT DONE.

IF THE PIECE SEEMS TOO THICK, CUT THE SIZE DOWN, HOWEVER THIS SIZE WORKS WELL FOR ME. YOU CAN TRIM EXCESS WITH THE SAW. TILTING THE BED MAKES FOR A SAFER TRIM JOB. I GO INTO A GREAT DEAL OF DETAIL ON THIS LITTLE GUY, BUT IT WILL HELP YOU ON YOUR OTHER SANTAS AND ANY FIGURES YOU CARVE.

BEGIN ROUNDING THE CAP.

INCISE AND BEGIN WORKING ON THE FACE.

DRAW YOUR ARM LINE. INCISE AND CARVE AWAY THE WASTE. WATCH THE HELPING THUMB.

NOW THE ARM IS TAKING SHAPE.

CONTINUE TO WORK ROUNDING THE HAT.

BE CAREFUL WITH THE LITTLE BALL ON THE CAP.

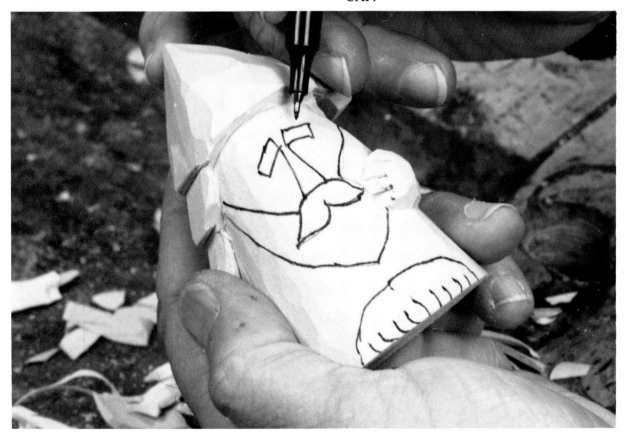

DRAW THE FACE AND BEARD LINES IN IF YOU'VE LOST THEM.

INCISE BETWEEN THE BEARD AND CHEEK AND
ROUND THE CHEEK.

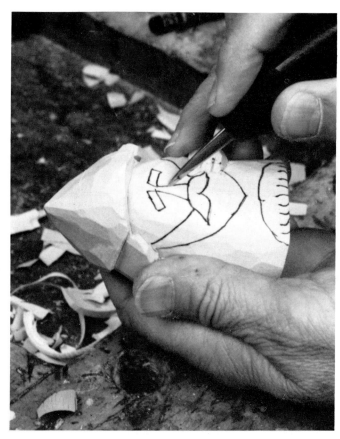

DON'T BE AFRAID TO CUT DEEPLY AROUND
THE NOSE.

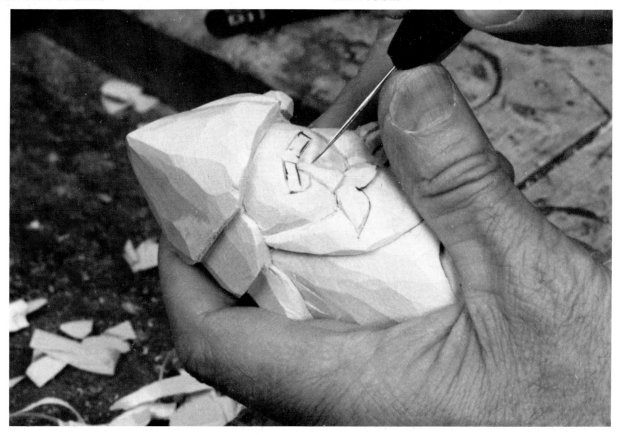

I'M CUTTING IN SOME BAGS UNDER HIS EYES.

ROUND, ROUND, DON'T LEAVE ANYTHING SQUARE.

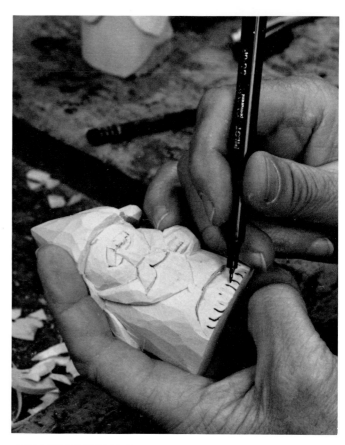

DRAW IN TOES AFTER YOU'VE CUT OUT AREA FOR TOES.

MAKE SMALL V CUTS FOR THE TOES.

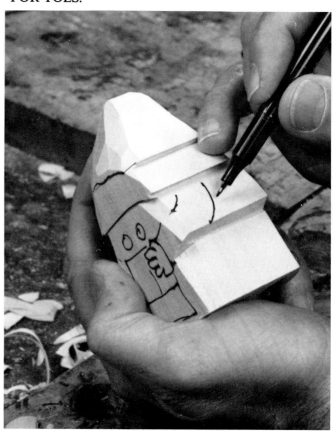

THIS IS THE RIGHT ARM. DRAW IT IN NOW.

CUT AWAY FROM THE RIGHT ARM—
CONTINUE TO GET THE ROUNDNESS ON THE
NIGHT SHIRT.

CUT UP TO THE HAIR LINE.

CUT THE CROOK IN THE RIGHT ELBOW AREA.

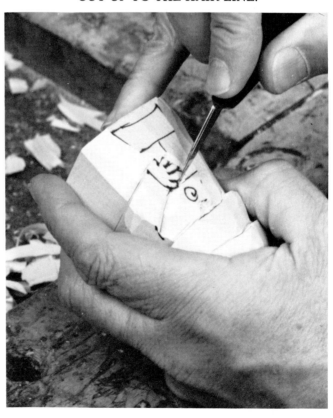

INCISE AROUND THE FINGERS. HE COULD
HAVE A MITTEN, BUT IT WOULD BE HARD TO
SCRATCH.

MAKE SURE YOU CAN STILL SEE YOUR LINES
ON THE FLAP AND THE VERTICAL BUN LINE.

DEFINE THE FINGERS AND FINISH THE AREA
AT TOP OF FLAP. CUT AROUND BUTTONS. YOU
MAY WANT TO BURN IN LATER.

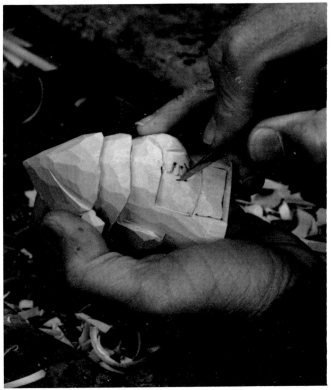

MAKE A 1/16" DEEP VERTICAL CUT.

ROUND THE CHEEKS ABOUT THE SAME AS
YOU DO THE FACE CHEEKS.

I HOPE YOU ENJOYED THIS SANTA AS MUCH
AS I HAVE. YOU ALMOST HAVE TO DO TWO SO
YOU CAN DISPLAY BOTH FRONT AND BACK.

SANTA WITH BEAR (D)

SOME FOLKS STILL HAVE TROUBLE WITH THE FACE.

AFTER YOU CHOOSE YOUR PATTERN, ROUND THE FACE AREA.

CUT DEEPLY AROUND HOOD.

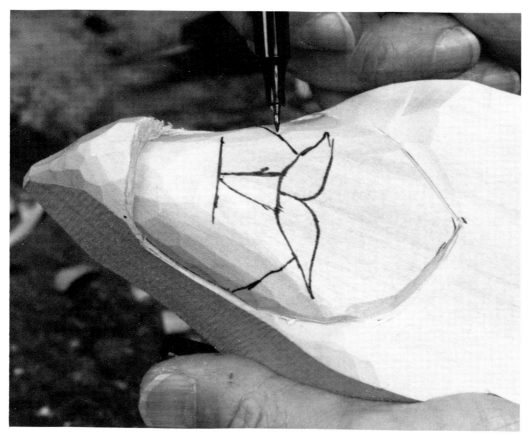

DRAW IN THE FACE. DON'T WORRY ABOUT
CUTTING YOUR LINES OFF. YOU CAN DRAW
THEM BACK.

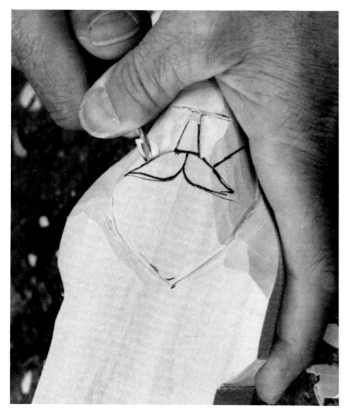

INCISE AROUND YOUR FACE LINES.

I WAS DEMONSTRATING TO GEORGE CLARK,
MY PHOTOGRAPHER, HOW TO FEEL THE
DEPRESSION MADE BY YOUR EYES.

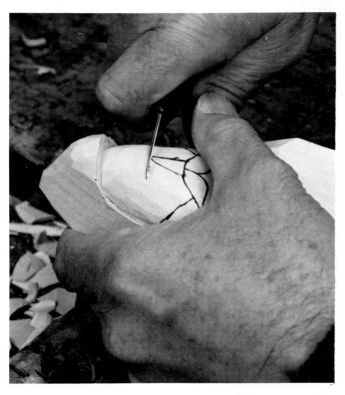

I CUT A HORIZONTAL LINE ACROSS THIS AREA FOR THE EYES.

CLEAN OUT THE CUT.

INCISE THE NOSE AND START DEFINING.

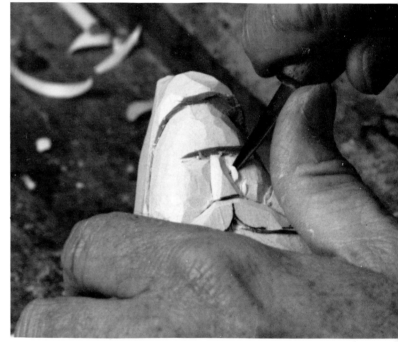

SEE THE NOSE BEGINNING TO TAKE SHAPE.
THIS IS THE REASON I DON'T SHOW A SIDE
VIEW EXCEPT WHEN THE SANTA IS IN PROFILE.

START TO ROUND THE CHEEKS.

THE BEARD IS BEGINNING TO TAKE SHAPE.

I THINK THE NOSE NEEDS A LITTLE MORE SHAPING.

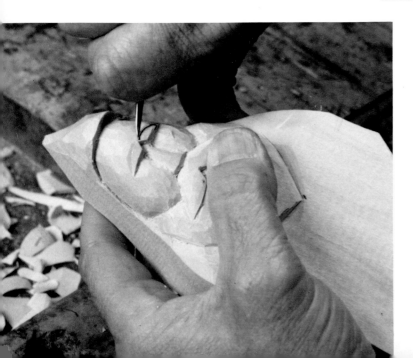

BE CAREFUL CUTTING THE EYEBROWS IN. YOU CAN GLUE THEM BACK ON.

I'M DETAILING EYES. NOT COMPLETELY
NECESSARY. YOU CAN PAINT IN THE EYES.

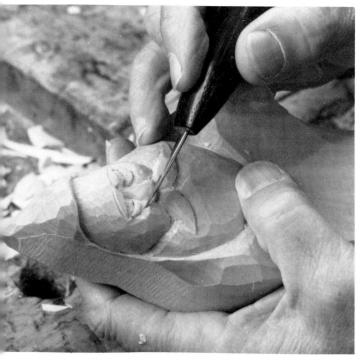

I'M PUTTING IN THE BAGS UNDER THE EYES. IT
TAKES A LITTLE PRACTICE, BUT YOU CAN DO
IT.

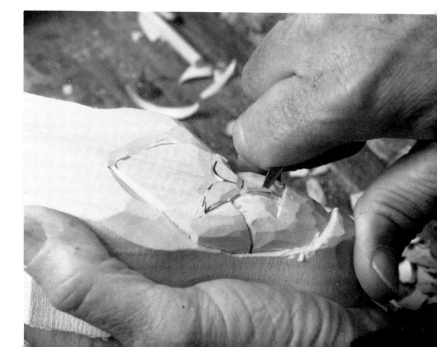

MOVE THE PIECE AROUND UNTIL IT'S
COMFORTABLE. I'M CARVING TOWARDS MY
THUMB. I NEVER DID GET MY MERIT BADGE
FOR CARVING.

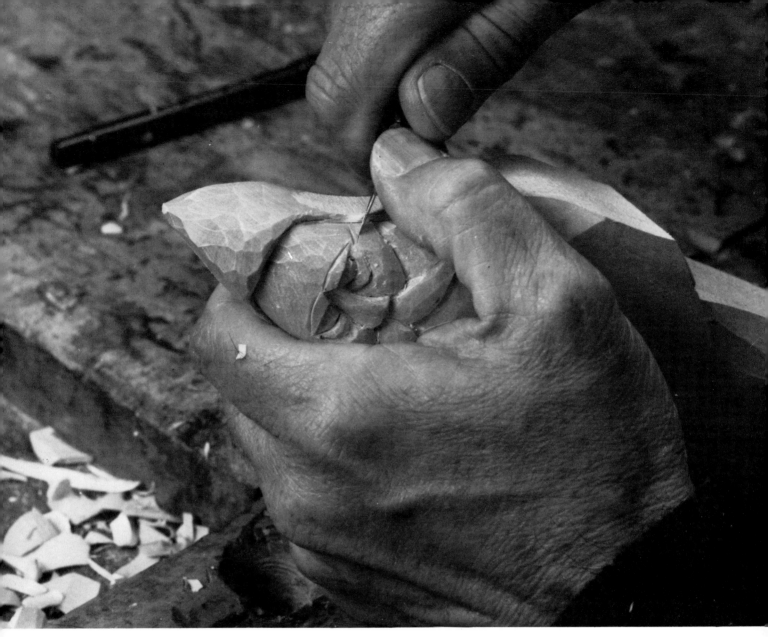

THE FINAL STEP ON THE FACE IS ADDING
CHARACTER LINES BY HIS EYES. I REPEAT
WHAT I TOLD YOU IN "SANTA CARVING". TAKE
PAINS WITH YOUR FACE AND THE OTHER
AREAS WILL NOT BE NOTICED.
   AS I TELL MY CLASSES, YOU DON'T LEARN
TO PLAY A MUSICAL INSTRUMENT IN A DAY
AND YOU WON'T LEARN TO CARVE IN ONE
DAY. PRACTICE, PRACTICE, PRACTICE.

Many of you have written for information on supplies, equipment, patterns and other things that would be of interest to carvers. I suggest that you join the National Woodcarvers Association, 7424 Miami Avenue, Cincinnati, OH 45243 and the National Carvers Museum Foundation 14960 Woodcarver Road, Monument, Colorado 80132. Their publications are super.

Some of you are having problems finding basswood. There are sources listed in these publications. I purchase my wood from Atlanta Hardwood Center 5322 S. Cobb Drive, SE Smyrna, GA (404) 799-8308.

I made a mistake (only one?) in the Santa Carving book by recommending a brand of shoe polish that is difficult to find. If you cannot find Griffin bark brown, try Meltonian which also comes in bark. It comes in a creame and works great. I found it at my local shoe repair shop. I did the design on the sweat shirt and had a few silk screened.

My first book was dedicated to my wife Evelyn and the grandchildren. In this photo she has made me leave the carving long enough to enjoy a Georgia fall day. Evelyn is my greatest supporter and toughest critic. If I get sloppy with my carving, she will call my hand. She is an antique dealer and a very good country decorator. We are in our thirty-sixth year of marriage and each year gets better.

PAINTING INSTRUCTIONS

THESE ANGELS WERE SOME
OF THE FIRST I CARVED.
THEY ARE DONE FROM
SUGAR PINE. NOTICE THE
HEART SHAPED BASES.

Angel #1   I HAVE PAINTED THIS ANGEL WITH BLUE HAZE CERAMCOAT BY DELTA.
THIS IS ACRYLIC PAINT. YOU USE ANY PAINT YOU LIKE. I'VE HAD GOOD
LUCK WITH THIS BRAND. ANTIQUE WITH GRIFFIN BARK BROWN OR
MILTONIAN BARK.

ANGEL #2
PAINTED WITH LILAC DUSK, FLESHTONE,
WHITE, KIM GOLD AND YELLOW HAIR.

ANGEL #3
PAINTED WITH CERAMCOAT SALEM BLUE,
WHITE, FLESHTONE, YELLOW HAIR AND KIM
GOLD FOR THE TRUMPET.

ANGEL #4
SALEM BLUE, WHITE, FLESHTONE, BROWN HAIR. I BURNED IN THE
FEATHERS.

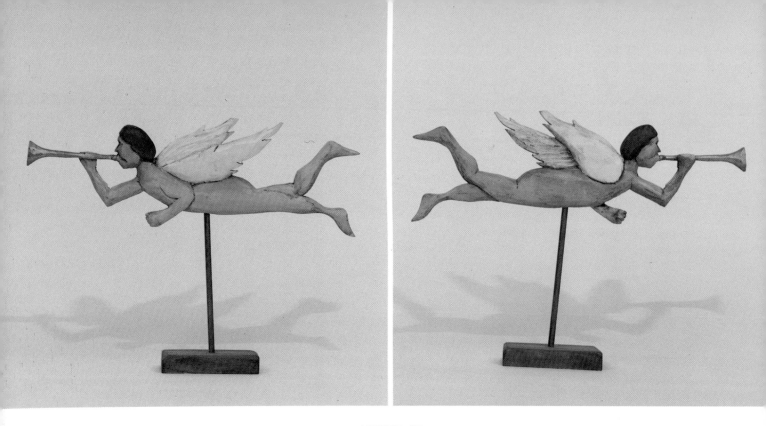

ANGEL #5
FLESHTONE, WHITE, KIM GOLD AND BROWN HAIR.

ANGEL #6
TOMPTE RED, WHITE, KIM
GOLD AND BLACK.

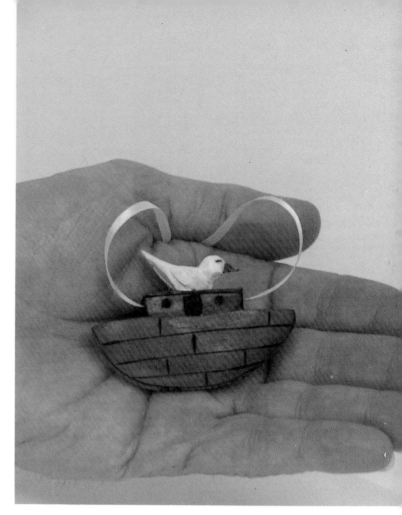

AN IDEA FOR YOUR NOAH'S ARK ANIMALS.
NOTICE MRS. NOAH HOLDING HER NOSE.

NOAH'S ARK NECKLACE WITH DOVE.

MY CAST SANTA MAKES A NEAT NECKLACE,
PIN OR HE WILL FREE STAND IF YOU GLUE
HIM TO A THIN PIECE OF BALSA. DON'T TRY
THIS ONE IF YOU'RE SLEEPY.

RANSOM '87

TREE SANTA (A)
YOU HAVE ASKED FOR DIFFERENT VIEWS OF
THIS SANTA. PAINTED WITH TOMPTE RED,
CHRISTMAS GREEN, WHITE, BLACK, AND
FLESHTONE.

FLYING SANTA (B)
MANY OF YOU ALSO WANTED MORE VIEWS OF THE WEATHERVANE
SANTA. COLORS ARE THE SAME EXCEPT ADD THE KIM GOLD FOR THE
TRUMPET.

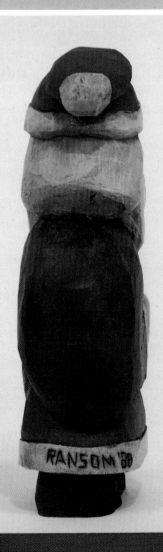

WALKING SANTA (D)
AS YOU CAN SEE, HE HAS HIS FACE LOOKING AT YOU. THE ARMS ARE
REVERSED. THE RIGHT HAND HOLDING THE BAG AND THE LEFT HAND
HOLDING THE STICK.

WALKING SANTA (C)
THIS SANTA IS INTENDED TO BE DISPLAYED IN PROFILE. USE THE SAME
COLORS. NOTICE THE BAG IS HELD IN THE LEFT HAND.

NIGHT AFTER CHRISTMAS
SANTA (E)

THE SANTA ON THE LEFT HAS BEDROOM SHOES. THE OTHER ONE IS BAREFOOT.

THE COLORS ARE NORMANDY ROSE FOR THE NIGHTSHIRT, WHITE AND FLESHTONE. I ADDED THE STRIPES WITH A PERMANENT RED FELT TIP PEN.

SANTA (F)
THIS IS THE SANTA THAT I USED TO
DEMONSTRATE FACE CARVING. I HAD AN
ORDER FOR THE BEAR AND SANTA. LEAVE
OUT THE BEAR OR ADD SOME OTHER ANIMAL.

SANTA (G)
WITH THESE VIEWS YOU CAN
DO IT. HE'S 10" HIGH.

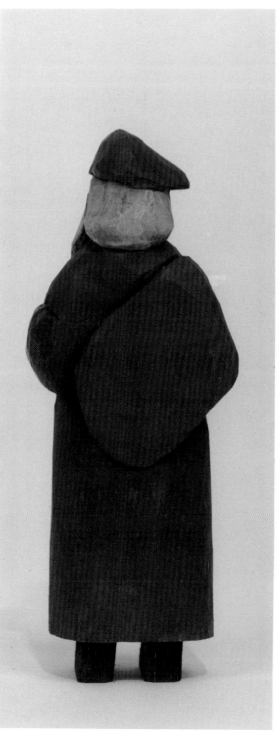

SANTA (H)

THIS PATRIOT SANTA
PATTERN IS IN "SANTA
CARVING." HERE ARE THE
OTHER VIEWS SOME OF YOU
WANTED.

RANSOM 1985
FOR EVELYN

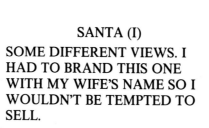

SANTA (I)
SOME DIFFERENT VIEWS. I
HAD TO BRAND THIS ONE
WITH MY WIFE'S NAME SO I
WOULDN'T BE TEMPTED TO
SELL.

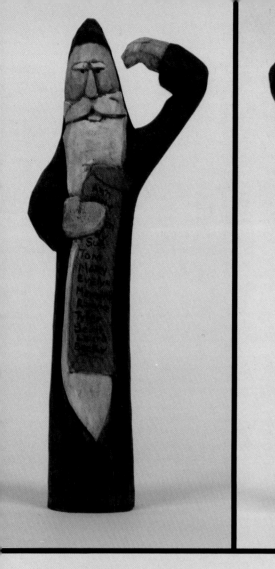

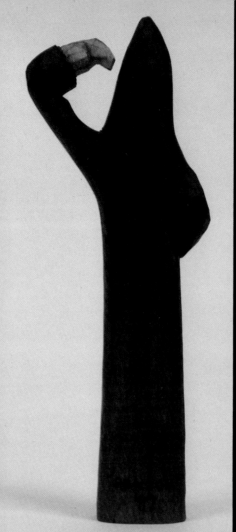

SANTA (J)
"WHAT AM I GOING TO DO WITH THIS LIST?" OR, "LOOK AT THIS MUSCLE, I CAN DO IT!"

MR. AND MRS. CLAUS (K) "MAMA, I HAVE A SURPRISE FOR YOU." "IF IT'S ANOTHER PEPPERMINT STICK I HAVE A SURPRISE FOR YOU." ONE REASON I DON'T DO MRS. CLAUS IS THAT THEY ALL LOOK LIKE JONATHAN WINTERS IN DRAG.

SANTAS (L) ALONG WITH THE TINY SANTA, I'VE HAD THESE THREE AND THE ANN & ANDY CAST. IF YOU THINK THEY WILL HELP WITH YOUR CARVING LET ME KNOW. THEY WILL BE UNPAINTED.

"THIS IS THE FUN ONE; TRY HIM LAST."